Adelma Grenier Simmons

THE WORLD OF
HERBS & FLOWERS

A Guide to Growing, Preserving,
Cooking, Potpourri, Sachets & Wreaths

Photographed by George Gregory Wieser

This book is meant to be educational in nature and is in no way meant to be used for self-treatment or self-diagnosis. Keep in mind that excess quantities of some herbs can be dangerous. The editors have attempted to include, wherever appropriate, cautions and guidelines for using the herbs and herbal recipes in the book. Yet, we realize that it is impossible for us to anticipate every conceivable use of herbs and every possible problem any use could cause. Moreover, we cannot know just what kinds of physical reactions or allergies some of you might have to substances discussed in this book.

For this reason, we cannot assume responsibility for the effects of using the herbs or other information in this book. And we urge that all potentially serious health problems be managed by a physician.

Herbs Are Forever

Caprilands' Guide to Growing and Preserving

Herbs Are Forever

Happy is the herb gardener through all the seasons and the years. That person enjoys a life enriched with rare fragrances at dawn, dusk and in the heat of noon. Each season bears an individual and special meaning, and each presents the gardener with gifts, uniquely its own.

From the bleakness of early spring to the richness of October, and far into winter, the herb garden continues. Long after the first frosts have destroyed summer's floral borders, the wreaths, vinegars, teas and jellies made from the preserved bounty of the garden warm the melancholy cold of the season and hint at the coming of spring.

Without moving from a sunny windowsill, or a chair by the fire, you may plant an herb garden as small or large as your imagination reaches. Plan and plant your gardens, sow your seeds, and enjoy your harvests. Make seasonings, vinegars, mustards, jellies, decorations, sweet jars and pomanders to suit your own needs, and whims, according to the size and shape of your herbal imaginings.

Drying Herbs

Drying home-grown herbs is one of the great pleasures of herb gardening. It is rewarding to use your own fresh seasonings to flavor your stews and casseroles throughout the year. Drying processes are simple, and the work need not be done all at once, for plants mature at different times.

Around St. Michael's Day, September 29, the busiest time of the drying season, Caprilands is decked in harvested herbs. Basil, savory, and mint hang from the kitchen rafters. Sage for holiday seasonings and flowers to add color to winter arrangements provide fragrant and beautiful table arrangements while drying for later use.

Culinary herbs are bent into wreaths and hung in the kitchen, to be picked as needed throughout the winter. The air is filled with good harvest smells and with the opening of the kitchen door the heady incense of heated spice and baking herb bread is wafted through the house.

Rosemary

Tender perennial, 3 to 6 feet. Needle-like leaves vary in color from gray-green to dark green. The blossoms may be white-rose or pale lavender. Root cuttings in sand or vermiculite using 3 to 4-inch pieces of new wood or healthy tips. Prefers full sun to partial shade with evenly moist, well-drained and alkaline soil.

Cut plants before noon, after the dew has dried but before the sun has leached the essential oils. Wash quickly in cool water. Spread leaves thinly on a tray of fine wire mesh and place in a slow oven (heat should not exceed 150 degrees). Drying should be completed within a matter of minutes. Dried rosemary needles are sharp if left whole; I run these through a coffee grinder and they emerge at just about the right length for coating a chicken, seasoning a gravy, or spooning out for tea. Store out of sunlight in an airtight container. Herbs to dry in trays include chervil, lovage, myrrh, lemon verbena, parsley, and thyme.

Caraway

Hardy biennial, 1 to 3 feet. Furrowed stems with finely cut leaves. Umbels of white flowers. Sow seeds in September for an early spring crop of leaves and seeds the following summer. Prefers full sun and average, well-drained garden soil.

Harvest the whole plant immediately after heads are mature. Place it, seed head down, in a paper bag so as to catch all the seeds. Hang up until dry and the seeds will drop out readily. Be vigilant and harvest promptly or seeds will fall to the ground and be lost. Herb seeds to dry include those of coriander, cumin, dill and fennel.

Oregano

Hardy perennial, 2 feet. Leaves dull, gray-green, oval, flowers pink, white or purple. Propagate by division of established plants in the spring, by rooting cuttings, or by sowing seeds. Prefers full sun and average garden soil, on the dry side and always well-drained.

Harvest herbs at noon and wash in cool water. Tie in loose bunches which are decorative hung from ceiling rafters or strung on a pole across the front of a fireplace. Be careful, however, not to let them collect dust. Dry in the shade, but not in a damp place, as this will slow drying time. Remove leaves from stems and store in airtight jars.

Other seasonings that dry well in bunches include sage, savory, mint, marjoram, basil, lemon balm, and horehound.

Christmas Confetti Casserole

3 medium onions, sliced
1 cup celery, chopped
1/4 pound butter
1 teaspoon dried basil
1/2 teaspoon dried marjoram
1 cup fresh parsley, chopped
1/2 teaspoon black pepper, freshly ground
1/2 cup pineapple chunks
4 pimentos, chopped
6 cups rice, cooked
1/2 cup almonds, blanched and slivered

Prepare the sauce by cooking the onions and celery in the butter until soft. Add the basil, marjoram, half the parsley, and the pepper. Stir in the pineapple and pimentos. Pour the sauce over the rice, and fluff with a fork until the rice is well coated. Correct the seasoning as needed. Put in ovenproof casserole. Spread the almonds over the rice, and sprinkle on the rest of the parsley. Hint: For an all-in-one meal, add 2 cups chopped, cooked chicken or tuna fish to the sauce. Add chives from the window box; dried parsley also may be used. Bake in 350 oven for 30-45 minutes until hot and bubbling. Serves 8-12

Freezing Herbs

Freezing is a simple process and most effective for sorrel, basil, parsley, dill chives, mint and chervil. Wash these lightly, then place on paper towels to drain and dry thoroughly. Do not blanche these leafy herbs as it has a tendency to make them soft and it is not necessary. Freeze separate leaves or whole branches in plastic bags as you do with parsley. Do not overcrowd the herbs, and be sure you lay them flat. Keep them frozen until it is time to use them. It is best, when freezing, to determine how much is usually used at a time in order not to waste the precious leaves. Herbs that are commonly used together may be frozen in the same packages. Be sure that you label each kind and pack them together. Unless you are very accustomed to their appearances, they can be confusing.

Mint

There are many, divergent types of mint, ranging from pineapple, to orange, from pennyroyal to peppermint. Their various uses range from spicing May punch bowls to warding off insects. Mint is a hardy perennial with divergent leaves but normally leaves are dark green, sometimes velvet sometimes smooth, and often splotched white. Stems often turn purple in the fall. Blossoms range from gray-white to pale purple.

Mint will grow almost anywhere. They thrive in humusy soil in shade, but also in sun and few pests ever bother them. Propagate from cuttings in spring. The only problem with mints is that they spread too rapidly, over running other plants and growing into a mass instead of staying in neat separate clumps. To avoid this, it is suggested you plant each clump of mint in a metal barrel, with top and bottom removed and sunk 18 inches into the ground.

Mint is cut in summer to make jellies, vinegars, and an essence for lamb sauce. Leaves are candied and also dried for teas. One method we have found very attractive for punch is to freeze small sprigs of mint in a cube of ice. The cube, when removed from the freezer will melt, leaving the herb ready to use, or if left frozen makes an attractive and useful garnish for the punch bowl. You can also freeze borage flowers, violas and tiny marigolds, which are more decorative then flavorful with the ice cube method.

Orange Mint Punch

1 cup orange mint leaves
2 tablespoons honey
2 cups water
6 tea bags decaffeinated tea
12 cups boiling water
12 ounces orange juice

Mix mint, honey and two cups water in a large saucepan. Simmer over low heat for 10 minutes. Remove from heat. Add tea bags and boiling water to mint mixture. Allow to cool for about 1/2 hour. Remove tea bags, then add orange juice and mix well. Refrigerate until cold. To serve, pour orange tea over a cube of ice with a mint sprig frozen inside.

Sorrel

French sorrel is a native of southern France, Switzerland, and Germany. It is a hardy perennial, 2 feet in height. It resembles the related and common dock of the fields. Leaves are succulent, long and shield-shaped, a light green color, sometimes veined with red. Flowers are like dock but smaller, softer in appearance, and a warm red-brown color.

Prefers sun to partial shade in rich, well-drained soil. Buy a plant, then allow it to multiply. It is difficult to obtain seeds of the true variety. Broad leaf garden sorrel is a good substitute.

Cut early in the spring and freeze leaves for later use in the year. At Caprilands, we freeze sorrel in large quantities for sorrel soup and bouillon. In our experience sorrel loses a little of its tangy sharp taste during processing. When substituting frozen sorrel for fresh in a recipe, it's best to use somewhat more than the fresh herb called for. Freeze sorrel leaves in plastic freezer bags.

19

Parsley

Curly parsley is a hardy biennial usually cultivated as an annual. It has bright green, tightly curled leaves. Italian parsley, also a hardy biennial cultivated as an annual, has large, fern-like leaves.

Parsley prefers full sun or partial shade in humusy, moist soil. To grow from seeds, broadcast or plant in shallow drills in well-prepared soil. Sow in midsummer for autumn cutting and to have small plants to bring inside for winter window boxes; for an early summer crop, sow seeds in earliest spring.

Parsley can be dried or frozen. Freeze either by the ice cube method in sprigs for garnish, or, as one of our assistants does, whose experience with herbs is of long standing, freeze in a ball and then shave off the desired amount as needed.

Herbal Teas

The tea ceremony is a ritual not only for the Oriental and the English, but for herb gardeners and their friends the world over. The connoisseur of tea finds the garden, the woods and the fields filled with leaves and blossoms to lend their essences to fine brews.

For me, herb tea will always be associated with winter sunsets. Others have a cup ready on the kitchen table to sip during a busy day, or remember special times when, in a shadowy old house on a wet spring day, with the garden practically swimming, they have spent a pleasant hour drinking tea from an old brown Staffordshire.

Camomile

Camomile is a creeping perennial, about 1 inch high, except to 12 inches while in bloom. Foliage is fine and fern-like. The flowers are white daisies with yellow centers.

Camomile prefers sun to partial shade in moist, well-drained soil. Sow seeds in spring or fall, or purchase plants. Once established, camomile will self-sow.

The mature flowers of two plants, Chrysanthemum parthenium and Antheis nobilis, are harvested for tea. The petals disappear when dry and only the yellow seed heads remain. They yield a slightly bitter brew that is refreshing for headaches and nausea, good for the nerves, and soporific. This is a household medicine and one of the most popular drinks in Europe. Allow a heaping teaspoonful of the seed heads to a cup of water; brew in a teapot. Strain before serving.

Calendula

Calendula officinalis is a small-flowered, Mediterranean plant from which the large-flowered garden hybrids came. The flowers, of varying shades of yellow and orange, open and at dawn and close in the evening.

Calendulas are annuals and may be sown from seed in the fall. They bloom more quickly in rich soil They will survive light frost. When harvesting, pick them at noon when they are fully open.

I use this herb, with mints, in making tea. In the past it was used as an aid to complexion beauty, and is said to be healing to the heart and good for the spirit. Both the large and small-flowered varieties make a good tea and add bright color to herbal mixtures. I dry calendula blossoms all through the summer and even into late fall, for they often bloom after frost has killed every other flower. I store the dried petals in airtight jars and have them ready to use in tea mixtures at the rate of 1/2 teaspoon per cup.

Lemon Balm

A hardy perennial, 1 to 2 feet, with branches grow-ing on a square stem. Leaves broadly heart-shaped, toothed, 1 to 3 inches long. Flowers inconspicuous, white or yellowish, off and on from June to October.

Lemon balm grows freely in any soil, but best in a well-drained location. Needs sun half a day, but will grow in shade. When plants are in a flower border, they need to be cut back to keep the foliage a good color as it has a tendency to turn yellow after flower-ing. Propagate by transplanting self-sown seedlings, or by sowing seeds (germination is slow).

I prefer to use lemon balm green for tea, but dry will also work. Pour 1 pint of boiling water over 1 ounce of the leaves. Let this steep for 10 minutes. Strain. Sweeten with honey. Lemon balm tea is rec-ommended for feverish colds.

Mint Tea

Mint is the herb most associated with teas. It is the strongest of the flavors and in its own right without other herbs, makes a good drink for those who wish to replace China tea or coffee as a beverage. Apple mint makes an especially good tea. We cut it about three times in the season and store the leaves in air-tight cans and in the winter, use it in concert with other herbs, or on its own. Pour 1 pint of boiling water over 1 ounce of leaves. Let this steep for 10 minutes and strain.

Herbal Oils and Vinegars

Throughout the summer our visitors at Caprilands are intrigued by the presence of gallons of what appears to be water, placed in the garden, among the plantings of basil, tarragon, mints, dill and chives. This is distilled vinegar waiting for the herbs to be placed in it as they mature.

As plants are harvested, we place leaves in a bottle of the vinegar and allow it to steep in the sun. After a week, the vinegar is ready to be stored in a cool cellar where it sits until it is time to place it in smaller, individual bottles. It then comes to the kitchen where it is strained to remove old leaves and any sediment. We pour it through a funnel into smaller containers that may come directly to the table. We place a piece of fresh herb in each bottle to add a decorative and extra added freshness to the final bottling.

Preserving herbs in cooking oils provides cooks with excellent assistance in food preparation. A bland, flavorless oil is a good medium for herbal flavorings. When herbs are fresh, it takes about two weeks for them to permeate the oil with their essence; if they are dry, allow a longer time, another two weeks. This process may be hastened by heating the oil to the boiling point before pouring it over the herbs. It will then make a good marinade for meat, for some salads, or for frying.

Opal Basil

Annual, to 2 feet. Leaves 1 to 2 inches long, shiny dark purple. The flowers are purplish in spikes. If spaced four inches apart in a row, each plant will grow like a small shrub.

Prefers sun to partial shade in average, but moist garden soil. After the weather has warmed in the spring, sow seeds where the plants are to grow

The tops of rapidly growing basil are cut frequently for if the top rosette of leaves is removed, the plant sets about growing a new crown of leaves immediately. It also grows new branches. The harvested leaves are placed immediately in the vinegar until the bottle is three-quarters full. Then it receives three top cuttings of dark opal basil, for color. This will, within two days ,tint the whole gallon a beautiful grenadine pink. Opal basil produces lasting color even when it is exposed to the sun.

Salad Burnet

Hardy perennial, 1 to 2 feet, evergreen. Leaves bear a similarity to those of the wild rose and remain nearly flat on the ground until flowering time. Flowers deep, but pale crimson in a round head.

Prefers sun with well-drained, alkaline soil. Sow seeds in late fall, early spring, and summer to have tender salad greens all year. Difficult to transplant except as a small seedling.

This is one of the most decorative of herbs and also flavorful. Place harvested leaves in a neutral cooking oil and allow to steep for two weeks for use as a marinade.

Dill

Hardy annual sometimes classified as a biennial, 2 to 2 1/2 feet. The plant is upright, branching out from a single stalk with feathery leaves and numerous yellow flowers in flat, terminal umbels, followed by dill seed in midsummer. The seeds are pungent tasting and retain their potency for three years or more.

Dill prefers rich, sandy, well-drained soil in full sun. Propagate by sowing seeds in the spring. If all seed heads are not harvested, dill may self-sow.

Use the large unbels to make herb vinegar. Dill in a sea green container is like an undersea picture and is excellent in freshly-mixed salad dressing.

Basil Vinaigrette

1 cup honey
parsley, rosemary, chives, thyme, basil
4 cloves garlic, crushed
1/2 cup basil vinegar

Add the herbs to the honey until it is thick with herbs. Mix with vinegar to make a dressing of desired consistency and tang.

Preserving Ornamentals

Herbs, flowers, seed pods, berries and cones, fresh and dried, provide beautiful raw materials for holiday decorations, wreaths, table arrangements, potpourri and garlands. To make everlasting decorations, you can dry the material so as to preserve their shape and color.

The best time to pick material for decoration is late morning. By that time, the sun has dried the dew but hasn't leached out the colors or the essential oils that keep perfumes and leaves and petals looking fresh. Flower color is brightest when blossoms first open. Many flowers will continue opening after they have been cut, so make allowance for this. Berries often have to be dipped in a glycerin solution to preserve their natural color and heavy stemmed, woody plants should be bent into their desired shapes while still pliable.

Artemisia

There are many varieties of artemisia and all can be used in wreath making for different effect. Varieties include southernwood, sweet Annie and wormwood. The plants provide profuse quantities of feathery plumes for long lasting, fragrant dried material. Most have silvery foliage, but some are brownish gray or even yellow green.

Artemisias are more easily grown from cuttings and root divisions than from seed. Depending on the variety of Artemisia you have upon maturity, they can range in color from a lovely, warm brown to a creamy, almost white. Harvest them in the middle of September.

Hang bunches of stems in a dry, well-ventilated room, or drape in airy wicker baskets to give stems a gently curling shape. Artemisia makes a solid base for fragrant wreaths and provides an attractive background for small flowers. Long stems, when fresh and pliable, can be easily twisted into a crown, or you can tie or wire small bunches to a wreath frame. The tips of small branches add a lacy, delicate look to wreaths and other decorations.

Feverfew

This chrysanthemum is known in New England as Brides Button. Its bright green foliage is attractive winter and summer, and makes a good border if the tops are cut back frequently. The flowers are white with yellow centers and are a long time in bloom. The plant has an odor of daisies which is often described as a camomile fragrance.

Grown from seed or plants, feverfew will self sow and spread. Plant in autumn.

These flowers dry best when placed in a drying medium such as sand, borax, or silica gel. Spread a thin layer of medium over the bottom of a wide, shallow container. Place the flowers in the powder so that the blossoms don't touch. Gently pour the drying medium over and around the flowers until they are completely buried. Leave the containers to stand in a warm, dry room. LIft the dried flowers very carefully from the medium, and use a soft brush to clean away remaining granules.

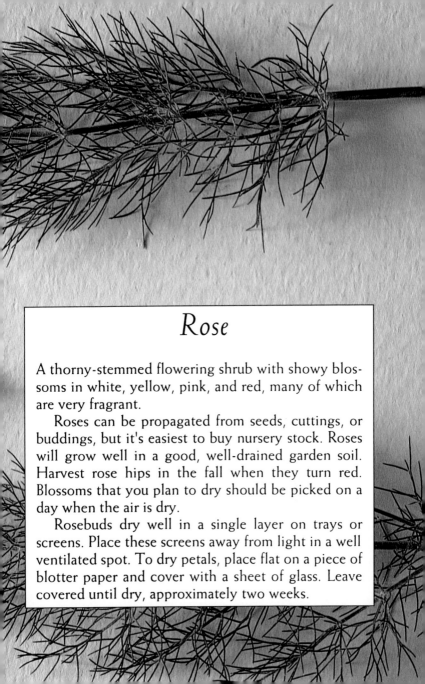

Rose

A thorny-stemmed flowering shrub with showy blossoms in white, yellow, pink, and red, many of which are very fragrant.

Roses can be propagated from seeds, cuttings, or buddings, but it's easiest to buy nursery stock. Roses will grow well in a good, well-drained garden soil. Harvest rose hips in the fall when they turn red. Blossoms that you plan to dry should be picked on a day when the air is dry.

Rosebuds dry well in a single layer on trays or screens. Place these screens away from light in a well ventilated spot. To dry petals, place flat on a piece of blotter paper and cover with a sheet of glass. Leave covered until dry, approximately two weeks.

Bride's Garland

Bride's Button
feathery ferns
ornamental grasses
florists wire

Bind together with fine wire blossoms and greens. Knot the wire firmly around the stems, take several turns around the length of the stems, and finish with a knot, but do not cut the wire. Position a second bunch over the stems of the first and continue, first tying a knot, then wrapping the stems, this time joining the stems of both bunches. Secure with a knot before adding a third bunch. Proceed until the flower rope is of desired length.

The Pride of Cooks

The Pride of Cooks

Herbal Recipes from the Caprilands Kitchen

The Pride of Cooks

Through the centuries, man has explored and recorded his findings in the world of herbs. Herb lore was collected by men and woman in all walks of life—physicians, poets, monks and housewives handed down a world of herbal knowledge on what can cure us, what can promise a bountiful harvest, the return of an errant love, or a tasty soup or salad.

All of us who study, write, talk about, grow or cook with herbs owe a great debt to the past, for herbal history invests even the most humble stew with an aura of romantic legend. Every season in the garden brings a new set of recipes, old and new to our kitchen at Caprilands. Spring, summer, autumn and winter-all have added meaning, for to each season the garden yields a special taste and presents a picture uniquely its own.

Tender Spring

A New England Spring is always the intermingling of two seasons. Winter is reluctant to remove its icy hold completely, yet seems to have great moments of indecision, when spring peeps coyly in and disappears at a shake of old winter's whiskers.

It is an anxious time for those who garden. The melting glances of spring expose roots, and encourage a rush of green growth, which are delicious and long awaited as the first fresh taste of the young season, but also tender and vulnerable to sudden plunges in temperature.

There are chives, chive blossoms, Egyptian onion stalks, sweet cicely leaves and blossoms, parsley, violets and violet leaves. Sometimes, we are lucky enough to have camomile. Mint leaves at this time are green, or darkly purple, like the orange mint, adding a touch of vermilion to our spring picture.

Sorrel

Hardy perennial, 2 feet. Resembles the related and common dock of the fields. Leaves succulent, long and shield-shaped. Buy a plant, then allow it to multiply. It is difficult to obtain seeds. Prefers sun to partial shade in rich, well-drained soil. Use in sorrel soup, sparingly in salads, as a sauce for beef, or cooked with beet tops, spinach, or cabbage.

Sorrel Bouillon

(Herbs— green sorrel, garlic, thyme)

1 handful of sorrel
1 clove garlic
3 grated onions
1/8 pound butter or margarine
6 cups chicken stock
3 large tomatoes
1 cup tomato juice
1/8 teaspoon thyme

Brown onion, sorrel and garlic in butter. Add stock and cook for 1/2 hour. Add tomatoes, (mashed or diced) and tomato juice and thyme, heat thoroughly. Strain if you wish to have a clear soup.

Calendula
(Pot Marigold)

The flowers, varying shades of orange and yellow, open at dawn and close at dusk. Grow pot marigolds from seed in rich soil. Prefers partial sun and will survive light frost. Lovely as a garnish or to add a light, fresh flavor to biscuits and soups.

Marigold Biscuits

1 cup fresh calendula flowers
  (pot marigold, or 1/2 cup dried)
1/4 cup chopped parsley
1 recipe baking powder biscuit dough (See cheese
  and sage biscuits recipe).

Add the calendula flowers and parsley to the biscuit
dough and bake as usual. Makes 2 dozen.

Fennel

Perennial sometimes grown as an annual, 4 to 5 feet.
The stems are blue-green, smooth and glossy, flat-
tened at the base; leaves, bright green and feathery.
Yellow flowers are produced in umbels. Propagate
by sowing seeds in the spring after the soil is warm
in full sun in average garden soil. Tender leaves and
stems in relishes, salads, and as a garnish. Use leaves
for flavoring in fish sauces, soups, and stews. Use
ripe seeds to flavor puddings, spiced beets,
sauerkraut, spaghetti, soups, breads, cakes, candy,
and beverages.

Fennel and Escarole Salad

1 head escarole, cut into small pieces
1 large bunch fennel, cut finely to make 4 cups
6 stalks celery, finely chopped
2 green peppers, sliced
12 artichokes
4 hard-cooked eggs, cut in quarters
1 cooked Italian sausage, sliced
6 slices Italian mozzarella cheese, cut into strips
1 cup onions, chopped

Toss the above ingredients together and dress with a French dressing.

Sumptuous Summer

When the drowsy heat of summer hangs over the hillside herb garden, there is little time to do more than keep up with all the cooking, weeding, harvesting and story telling duties that present themselves in the height of the season.

The garden is bursting with sweetness. There is peppermint, apple and rose geraniums, rosemarys, thymes, lavenders, and a tall lemon geranium, to add zest and depth to our midsummer menu.

Caraway

Caraway is a hardy biennial, 1 to 3 feet in height with furrowed stems and finely cut leaves resembling the carrot's. Umbels of white flowers appear in June of the second year. Caraway prefers full sun and average, well-drained garden soil. Sow seeds in September for an early spring crop of leaves and seeds the following summer.

Caraway oil is extracted from the leaves and seeds. Young leaves are sometimes used in soup; seeds, in applesauce, apple pie, cookies, cakes and breads. The oil is used in perfume, soap and in making a liqueur called kummel. The thick, tapering roots, similar to parsnips but smaller, are considered a delicacy for the table. Harvest the brown crescent shaped seeds before they fall to the ground and before the birds begin to eat them, usually in August.

Rose Cookies

1 cup butter
1/2 cup honey
2 eggs, beaten
1 1/4 cups unbleached flour
1 1/2 cups whole wheat flour
1 teaspoon baking soda
1/2 teaspoon cream of tartar
2 tablespoons rose water or 1 teaspoon rose syrup
2 tablespoons caraway seeds
raisins for garnish

Preheat oven to 375. Cream together butter and honey. Add eggs and beat well. Sift flours with baking soda and cream of tartar. Add to creamed mixture. Stir in rose water or rose syrup and caraway seeds. Drop mixture by teaspoonfuls onto greased cookie sheets. Flatten slightly with moistened fingers and put a raisin in the center of each cookie. Bake in a 375 oven until lightly browned, about 8-10 minutes. Remove from cookie sheets and cool on a wire rack. Makes about 8 dozen

Thyme

Many varieties of thyme exist today. Some are dark green; others are more gray or yellow, some creep; others grow upward. Several have a distinctly citrus fragrance, but all have tiny oval leaves and many branches that grow close to the ground.

Thymus vulgaris is the common thyme used to season foods. Thyme is a perennial and may be grown from seed on one season. Creeping thymes grow best from plant divisions. All need sun and good drainage. Harvest thyme when dew has dried off. Thyme is used as a seasoning in poultry stuffing, seafood dishes, stews, and cajun recipes. It is often combined with rosemary, parsley and sage.

Summer Squash Soup

3 medium summer squash (yellow preferably)
4 cups chicken stock
1 cup chopped celery
3 medium onions, thinly sliced
1 clove garlic, crushed
1 sprig fresh rosemary, minced
1/2 cup chopped parsley

Wash, trim, and slice squash. Steam the squash until it is tender. Puree the cooked squash in a blender or a food processor and set it aside (about 1 1/2 cups puree). Bring the chicken stock to a boil in a large saucepan. Add celery, onions, garlic, rosemary and thyme and simmer, covered, about 10 minutes or until vegetables are tender. Reduce heat to low, add reserved squash puree and parsley. Cook to heat through. Yields 7 cups

Sweet Basil

Basil is a favorite kitchen herb that has a clove-like odor and flavor. Its bright green, toothed leaves are very fragrant, especially in the sun, but they wilt quickly. Its many varieties include small-leafed, bush, lemon, purple (also called dark opal), and cinnamon.

Basil is an annual that grows easily from seed and likes the hottest weather. Sow seeds three times during the year for a constant fresh crop during the summer months. It likes a rich soil, although it grows well in average soil. To keep basil growing, harvest from the top to prevent plant from going to seed. The seeds come very quickly during the growing season, so cut the plant once each week.

Use leaves in salads, vinegars, spaghetti, soups, with meat, game, fish and tomato dishes. Excellent also in flower arrangements. Basil is often used in combination with oregano, olive oil and garlic.

Summer Salad

large basil leaves
ripe tomatoes, sliced
red Italian onions, sliced
green onions, chopped
chives, chopped
1 cup   honey
parsley, rosemary, chives, thyme, basil
4 cloves garlic
1/2 cup basil vinegar
sprigs of basil and green onions for garnish

Cover a platter with basil leaves. Arrange slices of tomatoes and onions so that they overlap. Spread the chopped onions and chives on top.

Add the herbs to the honey until it is thick with herbs. Mix with vinegar to make a dressing to pour over. Garnish with sprigs of basil and green onions. Hint; This salad is best when the tomatoes are really ripe and the basil leaves are crisp and prolific-late July and August at Caprilands.

Abundant Autumn

The herb garden in autumn has a special charm. Now that the competition of surrounding flower gardens is banished by the frost, the calm beauty of massed plantings of greens and greys is seen at its best. It is a time to appreciate leaf formation, texture, and the distinctive kind of growth that marks a green garden as a place for contemplation, delightful views, and mouth watering aromas.

The autumn kitchen at Caprilands is a season with many facets of interest and meaning. Modern lighting does not even completely break the spell, for the scent of the dying year is in the air and casts a curtain of magic over our tasks. Cutting a long row of sage, picking pungent pennyroyal, bunching thyme and stripping the fern-like tansy so that our garden's abundance can flavor our winter stew when this year's garden is but a fond memory in front of a fireplace.

Oregano

Oregano, also called wild marjoram, comes from the early name organy, because of its use in hot bags as an application for rheumatic swellings. It is a hardy perennial, 2 feet. Leaves are dull, gray-green and oval, with stems often purple. Flowers are pink, white, purple or lilac. The most flavorful oregano is a small-leafed, almost trailing plant with white flowers. It is easily overrun by the coarser types and needs to be kept separate and wintered inside.

Oregano prefers full sun and average garden soil, on the dry side, and always well drained. Propagate by division of established plants in the spring. Note that sowing from seeds always produces considerable variation.

Oregano leaves, fresh or dried, are used in spaghetti sauce, sparingly in salads, on tomatoes, and in herb seasoning mixtures. Excellent when combined with basil, olive oil, and garlic.

Squash Casserole

1 Hubbard or any yellow squash
1/4 teaspoon oregano
1/4 teaspoon cinnamon
butter
2 tablespoons brown sugar
1 whole nutmeg, grated
salt
pepper

Bake squash in a 350 oven until flesh is tender. Scrape flesh from shell, dot with butter and mash. Butter a casserole and fill with a layer of mashed squash. Dot with butter, sprinkle salt, pepper and oregano, cinnamon and brown sugar. Add another layer of squash and repeat spicing. Sprinkle top layer with grated whole nutmeg. Bake at 350 until flavors blend and squash warms.

Chervil

Chervil is known as the gourmet's parsley. It is an annual, 1 to 2 feet. Leaves alternate, fern-like, and spreading. The plant resembles Italian parsley, though more delicate, and turns reddish in the fall. sIt has small white flowers in compound umbels.

Chervil prefers moist, well-drained soil in partial shade. Sow seeds early in spring for an early summer crop; sow again in late summer for a fall harvest and one in early spring. Self-sows year after year.

Use leaves in salads and soups, with oysters, and as a garnish. The curled variety is best to grow as it has the flavor of anise.

Chervil Soup

12 large potatoes
4 medium onions, finely chopped
1/4 teaspoon caraway seed
4 peppercorns
1/2 cup chopped fresh chervil
2 cups evaporated milk
salt
paprika

Boil potatoes until soft and mash. Sautee onions and half of the chervil until soft. Season to taste with caraway seed and salt. Blend evaporated milk into potatoes until you reach desired consistency, add onions and chervil mixture and heat. When ready to serve, garnish with remainder of fresh chervil and paprika.

Sage

Sage is a hardy perennial, 3 feet. Leaves are oblong, gray and pebbly, on stiff stems that become woody and gnarled with age. Flowers blue in whorls with lipped corollas that tempt the bees and humming-birds.

Sage prefers a sunny site with moist, well-drained garden soil. Seeds of common sage sown in early spring will produce fine plants for cutting by fall. Propagate in spring or early fall by dividing old plants.

Cut leaves of common sage at any time for cheese sandwiches, souffles, and stuffings. Use dried in sausages, with cheese, pork, poultry, to season stuffing in turkey, and as a tea.

Cheese and Sage Biscuits

1 3/4 cups unbleached flour
1 teaspoon salt
2/12 teaspoons combination baking powder
5 tablespoons butter
2/3 cup milk
1 cup grated white cheddar or swiss cheese
1 tablespoon dried, powdered sage
1/2 teaspoon oregano
1/8 teaspoon garlic salt
paprika

Sift flour, then resift with salt and baking powder. Cut shortening into dry mixture then add milk and stir carefully until the dough comes away from the sides of the bowl. Dip in flour and knead lightly for less than a minute. Roll it out on a board as you would a jelly roll and spread generously with butter. Sprinkle grated cheese, sage, oregano and garlic salt on top of the cheese and roll up in a long roll. Cut in slices and arrange in a long cake tin on waxed paper. Curl bottom edges under to hold cheese in. Sprinkle top with paprika and dot each piece with butter. Bake at 425 until golden brown.

A Caprilands Christmas

In winter the strong lines of the Caprilands farm house are seen against snow-covered fields and gardens. Although with the green garden at rest and spring planting still far away, we do have an occasional moment to turn our eyes and energies inward, but the excitement of the coming holiday season keeps up busy in the kitchen and dining areas as well. It is never too busy, however, to sit and sip a cup of fragrant herb tea and plan colorful and festive holiday menus.

Christmas is the peak of the herb gardener's year, a time of long preparation, great anticipation, and much excitement. Many of the herbs that we have dried and stored from summer's bounty will enliven our holiday table as we celebrate the season.

Camomile

English camomile is also known as ground apple. It was once considered the plant's physician as gardeners believed that planting this herb among dropping and sickly plants would revive them. It is a creeping perennial, about 1 inch high, except grows to 12 inches while in bloom. The foliage is very fine and fern-like. The flowers are white daisies with yellow centers.

Camomile prefers partial shade in moist, well-drained soil. Sow seeds in spring or fall, or purchase plants. Once established, camomile will self-sow. The dried flower heads are brewed for tea and are well known for relieving nervousness, neuralgia, headaches and nervous colic.

Caprilands Tea

Remembering the many virtues that herbs have and could contribute to our well being, I have mixed a tea of rich symbolism. If you drink it, theoretically you should enjoy these benefits: wisdom from mint, memory from rosemary, immortality and domestic happiness from sage, bravery from thyme, happiness from marjoram, a good complexion and a bright outlook on life from calendula, and soothed nerves and a good night's sleep from camomile. Furthermore, this tea tastes good. To make it, mix equal parts of the dried herbs and allow 1 heaping teaspoonful to 1 cup of boiling water.

Tarragon

A perennial with green, lance-shaped leaves that grow full and bushy along slender, low growing stems. Tarragon prefers a sunny location and well-drained, rich soil. Tarragon seed on the market is not that of the true seasoning tarragon, all catalogs to the contrary. Start tarragon from roots in spring.

Use leaves, fresh or dried, in poultry and egg dishes, in vinegars, tartar and bearnaise sauces. Tarragon is a very powerful herb, and should be used sparingly, and not in competition with other, more delicate flavors.

Rose Geranium

There are over fifty rose scented varieties of geraniums. True geraniums are hardy perennials, but must be over wintered indoors. Leaf shapes for geraniums vary greatly from lacy, to fan shaped, fern leafed or ruffled and textures range from velvet to sticky.

Most leaves in the rose scented group are distinguished by a deeply cut leaf, irregular, with a very sweet, pungently rose scent. Geraniums will thrive in full or partial sun but will need spraying in the house as both white fly and red spider like the thick leaves. Varieties include the camphor rose, the old fashioned rose, and the lemon rose.

Use the dried leaves in potpourri, sachets, or fresh as an unusual accent in cakes and cookies,or a distinctive garnish for salads or pastries.

Rose Geranium Pudding Cake

3 egg yolks
2 teaspoons lemon rind
1/4 teaspoon rose geranium sugar
1/2 teaspoon plain sugar
3 tablespoons flour
1/4 cup lemon juice
1 cup milk
3 egg whites, stiffly beaten
4 rose geranium leaves
1 pinch salt

Beat egg yolks until foamy and add grated lemon zest and sugars. Beat vigorously and add flour and lemon juice alternately with milk. Fold in the stiff egg whites and add a pinch of salt. Place four rose geranium leaves on the bottom of a buttered casserole and turn the batter over the leaves. Place in a pan of hot water and bake for one hour at 350. The bottom will contain a thick lemon spongy cake. This may be topped with whipped cream and decorated with a few geranium leaves.

Herbal Oils and Vinegars

Place harvested leaves from basil, tarragon, thyme, dill or chives in a bottle of white distilled vinegar and steep in the sun. After a week, the vinegar is ready to be stored in a cool cellar where it sits until it is time to place it in smaller, individual bottles. It then comes to the kitchen where it is strained to remove old leaves and any sediment. We pour it through a funnel into smaller containers that may come directly to the table. We place a piece of fresh herb in each bottle to add a decorative and extra added freshness to the final bottling. Spices such as garlic, allspice, peppercorns or stick cinnamon can also be added to these vinegars both for taste and appearance.

Preserving herbs in cooking oils provides cooks with excellent assistance in food preparation. A bland, flavorless oil is a good medium for herbal flavorings and is particularly recommended for those who are on a salt free diet. When the herbs are fresh, it takes about two weeks for them to permeate the oil with their essence; if they are dry, allow a longer time, another two weeks. This process may be hastened by heating the oil to the boiling point before pouring it over the herbs.

Herbs such as rosemary, mint and sage make excellent jellies to accompany meat dishes. Boil herb leaves to make a base, and prepare as with all jellies, with pectin and seal with paraffin to store safely.

Catalog of Culinary Herbs

Anise

Annual, 1 to 1 1/2 feet. Leaves finely cut, gray-green. Flowers white. Prefers sunny, well-drained soil enriched with compost. Sow seeds very early in spring. When the seeds are fully formed, cut heads into a paper bag. Use as flavoring for cakes, cookies, candies, applesauce, stews, liqueurs, and wines, and to impart fragrance to soaps, perfumes and potpourri. Use fresh anise leaves in salads as a garnish.

Bay

Tender perennial, 3 to 6 feet when cultivated in a pot or large tub. Elegant, smooth-barked tree, evergreen leaves, thick, smooth and dark in color. Flowers small, in clusters, seldom appearing in the North. Propagate by rooting cuttings in moist sand and peat moss; provide shade and a moist atmosphere. Rooting may take six months or more. Use leaves for seasoning in stews, in casseroles, and pates.

Borage

Hardy annual, 1 to 3 feet. Leaves oval, blue-green, and covered with fine hairs. Flowers star-shaped, heavenly blue and pink or heavenly blue or lavender. Sunny location with well-drained, moist soil. Sow seeds in late fall or early spring and cut back frequently. Pick young leaves and use in salads for their cool cucumber flavor. Float the flowers in cups of punch or fruit juice. To candy the flowers, cut fresh, dip in beaten egg whites, then in sugar and dry.

Chives

Hardy perennial to 1 foot, producing fountains of hollow, cylindrical leaves. Flowers range from pink to blue in star-like clusters on long slender stems. Prefers sunny, well-drained garden loam. Sow seeds in spring or fall. Takes a year to establish from seed. Cut the leaves for soups and salads from early spring on; use in cream cheese mixtures, with mashed potatoes, in hamburger, or with eggs in omelettes. Blossoms can be used to flavor vinegar by steeping in white vinegar. Blossoms and leaves are good in salads. Chives can be frozen or dried for winter seasoning.

Coriander

Annual, 2 feet. Leaves finely cut like parsley. Delicate flowers in umbels, rosy lavender, appearing in late June. Prefers full sun in well-drained, moist, and fertile soil. Sow seeds in early spring, and thin out seedlings while they are small. Harvest seeds as early as possible. Use in curry, in chopped meat, stews, sausage, gingerbread, cookies and candies. The green leaves are used in Mexican and oriental cooking.

Dill

Hardy annual 2 to 2 1/2 feet. Feathery leaves and numerous yellow flowers in flat, terminal umbels followed by seed in midsummer. Prefers rich, sandy, well-drained soil in full sun. Propagate by sowing seeds in spring. Harvest weed early in summer, chop fine and dry in a basket, turning often. Sprinkle on fish, salad and soups during the winter. Harvest seeds as soon as the head is ripe. Large umbels of green dill are used to flavor cucumber pickles and herb vinegars.

Fennel

Perennial 4 to 5 feet. Steams are blue-green leaves, bright green and feathery. Yellow flowers are produced in umbels. Prefers full sun in average garden soil. Propagate by sowing seeds in the spring after soil is warm. Use tender leaves and stems in relishes, salads, and as a garnish. Use leaves for flavoring in fish sauces, soups, and stews; ripe seeds to flavor puddings, spiced beets, sauerkraut, spaghetti, soups, breads, cakes, candy and beverages.

Lovage

Hardy perennial, 3 to 5 feet. Leaves dark green resembling celery in appearance, color and taste. Flowers small, greenish, in small umbels. Prefers partial shade in fertile, deep and evenly moist soil. May be propagated by division in early spring, or from seeds, if they are sown in autumn immediately after they have ripened. Harvest tender leaves for soups, stews, potato salad, salad greens, sauces. Blanch stems and eat as celery. The seeds, whole or ground make cordials and may be used in meat pies, salads, and candies. Oil from the roots flavors some tobacco blends.

Parsley

A hardy biennial cultivated as an annual. Bright green, tightly curled leaves. Italian parsley has large, plain leaves. Prefers full sun or partial shade in humusy, moist soil. To grow from seeds, broadcast or plant in shallow drills in well prepared soil. Cut all through the season, using generously in salads, soups, casseroles, and omelettes with other vegetables.

Rosemary

Tender perennial, 3 to 6 feet. Needle-like leaves varying from gray-green to dark green. Blossoms may be white-rose, pale lavender, pale or dark blue. Prefers full sun to partial shade with evenly moist, well-drained and alkaline soil. Root cuttings in sand or vermiculite using 4 to 6 inch pieces of new wood or healthy end tips. Use green or dried, sparingly on chicken, in gravy with lamb, in soups, stuffings, sauces, dressings, in jelly, and as a tea.

Salad Burnet

Hardy perennial, 1 to 2 feet. Leaves ear a similarity to those of the wild rose. Flowers deep, ut pale crimson in a round head. Prefers sun with well-drained alkaline soil. Sow seeds in late fall, early spring, and summer. Fresh leaves smell of cucumber and may e cut while tender for salads, vinegars, cream cheese, drinks, seasoning green butters, and as a garnish. They do not dry well.

Summer Savory

Annual, 1 to 1 1/2 feet. Leaves narrow, dark green, on stout stems turning reddish and purple in fall. Flowers pale lavender or pure white. Prefers a sunny location in well-drained garden loam. Sow seeds in early spring. broadcast in a wide, well-prepared row and mulch with salt hay to prevent weeds and keep leaves clean. Cut two or three times during the drying season before blossoms form. Use in cooking green beans, for all bean dishes in stuffings, with rice, in soups, gravies, and sauces.

Sweet Marjoram

Tender perennial to 1 foot. Leaves gray-green, rounded and velvety. Flowers in white clusters have knot-like shapes before blossoming. Prefers full sun in well-drained, alkaline soil. Sow seeds in carefully pulverized soil in the spring. Use fresh or dried in soups, stuffings for pork or lamb, and with eggs.

Top Onion (Egyptian Onion)

Hardy perennial, 3 feet, with succulent hollow stems, ballooned toward the top. Prefers full sun in well-cultivated, fertile garden soil. Cut the spears of the young leaves as they appear in the spring for salads and t use with sorrel soup. Use the bulblets like small onions or pickle as cocktail onions.

Violet

The English violet prefers partial to full shade in humusy, moist soil. Propagate by dividing well-established clumps after they finish blooming. Candy the flowers for use on tops of cakes. Use them fresh in punch. Violets are used in May wine along with strawberries, and there is violet jelly, violet sherbet, and even violet fritters.

World of Fragrance

World of Fragrance

Potpourri and Sachets from Caprilands

Capturing the
World of Fragrance

The fragrant things of the world have a special romantic appeal. To walk in a garden of aromatic herbs is a rewarding experience. For the fragrance herb gardener, there is the additional reward of collecting summer's bounty and bringing the garden inside for winter enjoyment in the form of fragrant potpourri.

Historically, potpourri was not just pleasant but necessary. Improper sanitation, and the fear of fresh air, made the smell of flowers and spices a welcome relief to mask the accumulated odors of the rushes covering the stone or earthen floors.

It was the duty of a proper housewife to make potpourri, sweet bags and pomanders. The rose jar was kept on the table in the best room, and, after the cleaning was done, it was opened and stirred to scent the room and freshen the air. Sweet bags, filled with lavender, lemon verbena, with herbs and spice mixtures, were fitted to the backs of chairs and placed in closets and linen presses. Sweet herbs were strewn on the floors of church and home.

Many recipes for fragrances have been concocted. Some of these recipes found their way into stillroom books and were treasured as family heirlooms. Others were included in popular herbals and have become our common inheritance.

In this, our Caprilands Stillroom Book, we have presented brief histories of the essential materials that compose potpourri, as well as directions for growing and preserving them. To this we have added a few old recipes for scented things, and some of our own which we think are especially pleasing. It is such a sad waste of the fragrant flowers and herbs of the garden to allow them to drop to the ground unheeded, when, with a little care you can enjoy their fragrance throughout the winter.

Midsummer Mints

There are few plants in the garden as loved and useful, or as despised as the mints. To know them is to love them-and to be wary of their bold entrances into every domain of the garden. Still it would be hard to face a springtime garden without the curls of mint pushing though the brown soil like hundreds of small green roses opening up to the new season.

As we walk through the garden we can smell the cool odor of mint everywhere. It is indisputably a plant for tasting and smelling in hot summer weather. In ancient Greece and Rome, mint was a scent used by rich and poor. It was the custom to rub tables with it before guests were seated. To scent a room, hang bunches of mint from open doors or archways where a breeze will release the aroma, or tie them to screen doors to send cool odors through the house. When you are entertaining, place a sprig of mint on each napkin at the table.

Mints make fine terrace or patio plants. They thrive in redwood tubs, in large clay or pottery containers, or in plant pockets in terrace pavements. In using mints this way, be sure to provide drainage and evenly moist soil. Clip them back occasionally.

Orange Mint

The Orange Mint is one of the most fragrant plants in the garden and certainly the sweetest of the Mints. The clean citrus scent combines with Lavender and Bergamot, which it resembles in color. It dries well, keeping a good green color.

Peppermint

Peppermint is too strong for the sweet jars, but is wonderful in a more medicinal type mixture that can be used as one uses menthol. Its prime value is to clear the head and use as the ancient scholars used the mints, to clear the brain.

Mint Geranium

The large velvety leaves of the Mint Geranium combine well with the true Mints in the making of a clean smelling somewhat medicinal (but pleasantly so) potpourri. The leaves retain their heart shape well when pressed and dried and are quite decorative.

Mint Jar
A Potpourri to Clear the Head and Speed Up Mental Processes

2 cups dried lavender
1 cup dried mint (mix equal parts orange mint,
    spearmint, mint geranium leaves)
1/2 cup dried culinary thyme
1/4 cup rosemary
few drops of essential oils of lavender, thyme and
    bergamot
dried red geranium petals, blue bachelor's-button
    and delphinium

Combine ingredients and store in apothecary jars. When you're entertaining, turn some of this mixture out into a pewter or silver bowl. Stir slightly to release the fresh scent. An excellent potpourri for a desk or worktable, perhaps in an antique sugar bowl.

Lemon Zest

Lemon varieties are among the most fragrant of garden herbs. There is no other odor that can match the lemons for freshness. The scent is reminiscent of such pleasant things as a Victorian house with high cool rooms, closed shutters keeping out the heat of the day, or a sunny day in a Guatemala, where one can fill one's pockets with the leaves of the native Lemon Verbena bush.

Lemon Verbena, came from the Southwest via the spanish conquest and eventually arrived in England in approximately 1784 where it was immediately accepted for the fresh, cool odor it imparted to fragrant preparations. Other lemon varieties, however, such as balm and thyme, appear in old still books as having "an admirable virtue to alter melancholy." They were most often steeped as teas to cure feverish colds and improve attitudes.

The Lemons make delightful patio plants. Place lemon plants in a tub where they can be brushed as people walk by to release their clean odor. Plant lemon thyme in the cracks of walk ways or patio stones so that its fresh scent is released as people walk. Often, lemon leaves were used fresh as a garnish for sponge cakes or set on a sill over a sink to treat the cook to a breath of the past, an odor from a far away place.

As the lemons come from a variety of species, growing instructions vary widely, according to the family to which it belongs. Lemon Balm is a hardy perennial which may be grown from seed, planted in either spring or fall, and self sows in some situations. It winters well. The lemon geranium can be planted outside as soon as the danger of frost has past. Scented geraniums must be wintered indoors. Lemon Verbena is a tender perennial tree. There is no readily available or viable seed, therefore most plants are grown from cuttings, and must winter indoors.

Lemon Verbena

There is no odor quite like that of the Lemon Verbena, which is known as Vervain, the herb of enchantment, in the south of France. The leaves are very fragrant, although their scent is somewhat transient. It is best when combined with Lemon Balm and Lemon Peel. Lemon Oil may also be added to renew faded odors. Leaves with a little scent will still taste good as a tea. It can grow as a topiary tree by training on a support stake and cutting the lower shoots so that one stem emerges to branch out at the top, making a fragrant umbrella of leaves.

Lemon Balm

Lemon Balm has a delightful odor, attractive to the bees, resembling Lemon Verbena with the added advantage that it will live over the winter. It grows into a small bush and the height increases in the second year to 2 feet or more. Its wrinkled leaf is very decorative in the early spring when it emerges from the ground, and can thrive in sun or shade. Lemon Balm is reputed to be a "Balm for troubled spirits," but also makes an excellent tea and the fragrant leaves retain their refreshing odor well when dried and therefore are a good addition to potpourri.

Prince Rupert Crispum

The Lemon Geranium is second only to the old fashioned Rose in the memories of those who attempt to reconstruct a garden of the past. Like the rose there are many varieties with this refreshing lemon scent, however the prince Rupert is the sturdiest, and the most lemon. During the space of one summer in the garden under even fair conditions this will become a small shrub. Put in decorative terra cotta pots and allow it to grow as large as it wishes. It can be a pleasant addition to a terrace landscape or a flower pot garden. Prince Rupert also makes a delightful addition to hanging basket arrangements, or window box plantings. While the scent is strongly lemon, it blends with other odors pleasantly.

Lemon Verbena Jar
It causeth the mind and heart to become merry

1 cup dried lemon verbena leaves
1 cup dried lemon balm leaves
rind of 1 lemon, dried and grated
1/2 cup each dried petals from forsythia, calendula,
    lemon geranium, lemon-scented marigold, lemon
    thyme
1 ounce orris root with 6 drops of lemon verbena oil

Combine all ingredients, then turn into small apothecary jars. Press some of the yellow flowers against the sides of the jar for color. Tie the top with yellow and green velvet ribbon.

The Lyrical Lavenders

Lavender is one of the most ancient fragrances. It came to England with the Romans and found its happiest home there. It was used by the Greeks and Romans much as we use it today: for its clean sweet scent in washing water, soaps, pomades and perfuming sheets. It was a strewing herb in medieval times and a medicine believed to cure 43 ills of the flesh and spirit. Lavender has always been used to attract the bees and it produces an epicure's honey. It was also reputed to be a preserver of virtue, and was often used in wedding wreaths and bridal crowns, as a symbol of the brides innocence and purity.

The entire Lavender family is highly scented. Both the leaves and blossoms are used, although the blooms give off the most odor and carry the characteristic color. Lavender used in varying amounts will improve almost all potpourri and is also useful for the color that it adds to a glass jar. Its clean odor may be the necessary cool element needed to clam an overpowering mixture.

Trying picking bouquets of the blossoms and placing them in vases and baskets in the house. They are not only decorative, but impart a lovely scent, and if the weather is not unseasonably moist, the flower heads will dry perfectly for later use. Cut the blossoms when they are fully out, or the color will fade. Lavender is also stuffed into divan or sofa cushions to keep furniture clean smelling, or tied in sprigs behind curtains to freshen the air. Small lavender pillows can be placed in the corners of drawers to sweeten linens.

It is best to start your Lavender beds from plants, although seed sown in the late fall or very early spring will usually produce some seedlings. Lavenders are hardy perennials. The varieties Vera and Spica are hardy as far North as Nova Scotia. Sun, lime and drainage are the three requirements for successful growing. In winter a cover of boughs of evergreen or salt hay is desirable.

Hidcote

A hardy variety of lavender with branched narrow leaves and a dark blue flower. This makes a fine ornamental border plant, and may even grow large enough to be used as an unclipped hedge. Hidcote is a lovely addition to a bee and butterfly garden, or a fragrance garden and dries well for use in many fragrant mixtures. Lavender blossoms were often used as a tisane to cure nervous headaches.

Jean Davis

A hardy variety of lavender with pinkish white blossoms. When combined with Hidcote, this contrast of colors makes a beautiful and fragrant border for any garden, and is also useful in dried and fresh lavender table arrangements. Jean Davis, like all lavenders is fragrant and delightful in potpourri, or braided into a permanently sweet smelling wreath.

Vera and Spica

The hardiest and most common of the lavenders, these are perennials even in New England and well worth growing. Their blossoms are blue and leaves a silvery gray. Sprays of lavender were used by the harvesters in England-worn under their hats they were thought to stop sunstroke and headaches caused by the sum.

Moist Potpourri

Lavender for lovers true

1 cup dried lavender
3 cups dried rose petals
1 teaspoon each of allspice, cinnamon and coriander
1 tablespoon each of cloves, grated nutmeg, and anise
1/4 cup each of patchouli leaves and powdered orris root
1/4 ounce each of oil of rose and oil of rose geranium
3 cups of a mixture made of dried rosemary, lemon balm, and lemon verbena leaves.

In a covered crock, mix rose petals with the bay salt and leave for one week, turning daily. Add spices and let stand for another week, turning daily. At the end of the two weeks add the lavender, patchouli, orris root, and oils. Let stand for a few weeks, then mix in leaves of dried rosemary, lemon balm, and lemon verbena. Stir frequently with a wooden spoon or cinnamon stick.

The Romance of the Rose

The rose, special flower of midsummer, has always been symbolic, generally,of love and romance, although in one of the later books on the Language of Flowers, there are forty entries for the meaning of the Rose ranging from love to shame, from youth to age, from war to tranquility. The rose became a symbol of war in the fifteenth century when it was adopted as the badge of the rival English Houses of York and Lancaster. Brides, and indeed both sexes in ancient times, were crowned with a chaplet of red and white roses, and instead of rice, were pelted with petals as part of the celebration.

Roses are highly prized for their value in fragrant mixtures. Rose petals are used in a wide variety of potpourri, both for their everlasting color and subtle scent. Attar of roses or rose oil, made from steeping roses in oil is indispensable in the creation of potpourri. Often only one drop is necessary to impart a fragrant and lasting odor to any blend. Rose water is used as an invigorating after bath splash, and in the preparation of many delicious dishes.

Roses can be propagated from seeds, cuttings, or buddings, but it's easiest to buy nursery stock. Roses will grow well in a good, well-drained garden soil. Blossoms that you intend to dry should be picked on a day when the air is dry. For perfect rose petals, pick before they are completely blown. Remove the petals and place them on a large sheet of blotting paper and cover with a heavy piece of glass. Leave until dry.

Rosa Damascena

The damask rose is associated with the famous "Valley of the Roses" in Bulgaria where hundreds of individual rose farmers cultivate this fragrant rose. Many of these distilled their own essences in old fashioned, primitive stills. It is said that it takes 10,000 pounds of damask roses to make one pound of oil.

Apothecary's Rose

One of the oldest varieties of roses referred to as a "June" rose, and known for its sweet and powerful fragrance. The apothecary's rose, like other old June varieties, such as the Damask, are so fragrant that they are used in the production of rose oil, and also can be combined as petals in potpourri that requires no essence. Although this is an heirloom variety, it is especially hardy.

Rober's Lemon Rose

This is a scented geranium, and not a rose proper, but this plant's long thick leaves have the sweetest of rose scents. Rober's lemon rose looks rather like a tomato plant as it starts growth. This plant is very hardy, and will yield hundreds of the sweetest leaves in the garden which may be used in potpourri or tea.

Rose Jar

To bathe young buds in dews from heaven

1 quart dried rose petals
1 cup each of dried lavender flowers and rose
    geranium leaves
1/2 cup patchouli
1/4 cup sandalwood chips and vetiver, mixed
1 teaspoon each of powdered benzoin, cinnamon
    and cloves
2 teaspoons frankincense and myrrh, mixed
2 tonka beans, ground
1/4 cup allspice
10 drops rose oil
1 cup orris root

Mix first eight ingredients thoroughly, then add the
rose oil and orris root. Mix again and stir well. If this
amount of orris seems excessive remember that this
is a base mixture to which you can add flowers of the
season right up to fall. After it is finished, close the
jar for at least two weeks (a month is better), then it
will be ready to enjoy.

The Sweet Sandalwoods

The odor of sandalwood is one of great fascination. It is reminiscent of the opening of a chest filled with oriental silks, or of an elaborately carved fan whipping the air in the hot moist atmosphere of an Indian jungle. It also recalls the Victorian parlors of New England. I shall never smell sandalwood without a momentary glimpse of this fascinating sanctuary of my youth.

This "sanders wood" of the old recipe books does not have a charm for all people. In fact, there are many who at first are unable to sense its faded, faintly spicy odor, though, if it is burned where it can penetrate and linger in the rooms, there are few who do not enjoy it. Sandalwood must be heated to make it the most odorous. Sandalwood chips are best for the purpose of maing potpourri, and they add that indefinable something to a jar. Blocks can be placed in drawers to keep clothes smelling fresh. The odor of sandalwood discourages moths.

White Sandalwood

White sandalwood is a small tree, 20 to 30 feet high and native to the Malabar coast. It is also found in New Caledonia. Though it has a growth potential of 30 feet, it seldom attains its full height, but remains a bush or a low growing tree. From early times, its wood was highly valued for its sweet odor. It was employed in the making of musical instruments, particularly those that were used in sacred ceremonies. It was also used for burning at the sacrifices of idols and was later a part of the incense used in the Jewish synagogues. For more domestic purposes, fans were made of it, and it was used to line boxes, to make chests secure against the inroads of moths.

Red Sandalwood

A large tree indigenous to Ceylon and India. The wood of this variety is very heavy and extremely hard, suitable for the making of long lasting carved furniture. It is still in use today in the production of such musical instruments as lyres and lutes.

Simmering Sandalwood

1 cup sandalwood chips or shavings
1/2 cup lavender flowers
1/2 cup rose petals
2 teaspoons frankincense and myrrh, mixed
1 teaspoon vetiver
1 teaspoon cinnamon
1 teaspoon allspice

Combine all ingredients and place in an apothecary jar. To simmer, place potpourri in a small pot with water and allow to simmer over a tea candle, or, place in a bowl with water and set it atop a radiator to steam scent the room in the winter.

Fixatives to Hold Flower Fragrances

Fixatives from the animal or plant world are used to hold the fragrance of potpourri ingredients. Animal fixatives include ambergris, civet, and musk. The odor of fixatives alone, in particular, ambergris from the sperm whale, is disagreeable, but when combined with fragrant things, it absorbs and enhances the essences.

The plant fixatives I use most are orris root, and tonka bean. Orris root comes from Iris florentina, a variety of I. germanica. The fresh root is dug, peeled and sun-dried, then stored for two years to develop the scent. It is then ground and emits the violet odor for which it is known. Orris root is the most common fixative for potpourri as it is easily obtainable.

Essential Oils

When essences or essential oils are included in recipes, the distilled plant oil is indicated. These are generally volatile oils that evaporate at room temperatures. They occur in secretory cells, reservoirs, glands of flowers, barks, fruits, and leaves. Most oils are obtained by steam distillation. A very common oil is Attar of roses or rose "otto" as it is sometimes called. Other oils used in the making of potpourri include oil of violet, carnation, jasmine, lemon verbena, and orange blossom.

Spices for Potpourri

Allspice: A member of the myrtle family native to the West Indies. Allspice adds a wonderful touch of bayrum to potpourri.

Calamus root

This product of Acorus calamus comes from France and Belgium. Calamus root, and the oil derived from it add a mellow and spicy odor to potpourri.

Cinnamon bark or sticks

A member of the laurel family which yields a spicy element which was once the chief ingredient in the manufacture of the holy oils of the bible.

Cloves

A member of the myrtle family native to Zanzibar, British Malaya, Ceylon, Indian, Madagascar, and Penang. The citrus scent adds a lovely orange touch to potpourri.

Frankincense

Native to the East, frankincense gives us the most used and treasured of all the sweet odors. The odor of frankincense is not discernible in potpourri, unless the mixture is warm or moist. However, it is a fixative and adds stability to a mixture.

Myrrh

Native to Arabia, the fragrant bark and gum is not only sweet smelling, but in the past was used to soothe a sore throat, and as a purifying agent.

Patchouli

Native to the tropics, these large, musk-smelling leaves give depth to potpourri and have fixative powers as well.

Tonka Bean

Native to Brazil and Ceylon, Venezuela, British Guiana and Africa, this bean provides one of the most concentrated of floral odors. It is overpowering in its sweetness, heavy with the smell of coumarin. The ground beans are important for good potpourri, since they act as a fixative and an intensifier, sharpening other odors while losing their own.

Vetiver root

Comes mainly from Java although small amounts do grow in Louisiana and the West Indies. It has a fragrant root with the odor of violets or sandalwood. As a fixative in potpourri, it never seems to lose its fragrance.

When to Make Potpourri

Through the summer and far into autumn, the good herb gardener is busy harvesting. Airtight tin containers hold chip-dry rose petals, aromatic lavender, lemon verbena, orange mint, and other members of the mint family. Large boxes or drawers in an old dresser hold a colorful selection of dried flowers, not necessarily fragrant, for decoration within the glass jars of potpourri.

It is important to keep drying material in a dry, well ventilated location, where air is able to circulate. Moisture must be avoided. Leafy materials can be tied in loose bunches and hung in a well ventilated place until dry. Petals can be placed on a sheet of blotting paper and covered with glass until dry.

The sun will fade the colors of the brightest, freshest lavender or roses, so keep potpourri jars and drying materials out of the sun or strong light, except on occasion.

How to care for Potpourri

Potpourri can be renewed several ways. A few drops of alcohol or brandy will revive a fading, fainting odor. Add a few patchouli leaves, some fresh lavender or drops of essential oils and extra spice will help also.

Removing the whole from the jar and remixing is the best way to restore it. Some new petals may be added with drops of oil. If you wish to make a new jar and discard the old, store the faded mixture in a tight container and burn it as incense. Although it may no longer have a strong odor when dry, if burned, it will smell as sweet as the Indies.

A mixture that will last in a jar for years will fade in a few months if put in a cloth or silk container. keep the bulk of your potpourri in a covered jar and use only a little at a time in bags.

Sachets and Scented Pillows

Sachets are made simply by tying up a fragrant dried mixture of potpourri in a square of organdy or fine net. Decorate with little dried roses or everlastings and a bow. Antique glass containers with a sachet in them make delightful gifts.

Covers for scented pillows are made of organdy, fine net, or silk, but put the more sturdy fragrances of pine and patchouli into soft felt or homespun. Pieces of brocade, velvet, and chintz also make useful covers. For these small pillows, make an attractive case of one of these materials and a slightly smaller lining of muslin to hold the fragrant mixture.

Use prolific plants from the herb garden for the bulk of fragrant material for pillows. Lemon balm is one of the most leafy herbs; lemon and camphor southernwoods also produce an abundance of foliage with a clean, penetrating and lasting scent. Combine any of these with cuttings of rosemary, bergamot, thyme and bay leaves, and a generous amount of dried orange and lemon peel.

A Year in Wreaths

A Year in Wreaths

Caprilands' Guide to Wreaths

Wreaths Through the Ages

In all eras there has been the longing for a return to simpler times, nostalgia for the basic, the natural, the homely virtues, the simplicity of the past. Never has this been more prevalent than in our complicated, modern world.

Wreath making is one of the ways we can return to a time when life was far more influenced by the seasons of the growing year, the bounty of the harvest, and the simple courses of nature.

Wreath making, throughout history, has been a way to celebrate the stirring of the seasons, and to mark holidays of personal, national or religious significance. To the ancient Greeks, wreaths were crowns of glory to signify victory, or wisdom. In the Middle Ages, wreaths marked saint's days and high church holidays. In agricultural communities, herbal wreaths expressed gratitude for the harvest, and hope for future bounty. Today, as in the past, wreaths, and the herbs of which they are composed, can enrich our appreciation of life.

St. Anthony's Nut

Celebrated on January 17, this festival, falling in mid-winter, was often celebrated with a feast of the meat salted earlier in the autumn. Meals may have included pork, as St. Anthony was the patron saint of pigs. The herb normally associated with St. Anthony is the Pignut, but as in most cold weather celebrations, fragrant herbs of all kind were employed in the decorations of the day.

Fragrance Wreath

Fragrant herbs such as rosemary, lavender, mint, lemon balm and sweet woodruff can be used either by themselves in elegant and fragrant wreaths, or placed in sweet bags of potpourri and attached to ornamental wreaths. Combine leaves from several lemon-scented plants into an attractive wreath or make a rosemary wreath that is fragrant and useful to the gourmet cook.

St. Dorothy's Day

The Feast of St. Dorothy is celebrated on February 6 and is associated with roses. Although normally a flower of midsummer, traditionally on St. Dorothy's day brides and other celebrants were crowned with dried rose chaplets, and pelted with rose petals. In some gatherings, showers of roses were a part of the celebration.

Rose Wreath

Rosebuds, which have been dried on a tray in a well ventilated and shaded environment, can be wired into a base of silver king or sweet annie, for a lacy look. Ribbons can also be tied into the base for an attractive and colorful accent.

Whitsunday

Whitsunday or Whit-Monday is the first of the spring festivals. In agricultural communities of the past, it was the time to gather the first blossoms of spring into the house, and express hope for a bountiful growing season. Green birch trees were often cut and carried in parades by Jack of the Green, who was thought to bestow blessings of the harvest. Lilies, birch and sweet woodruff were associated with this feast day.

Lily garland

Daffodils or other spring lilies, ferns and fragrant herbs such as sweet woodruff, may be bound into a long flower rope to adorn hallways or woven into chaplets which may be worn on the head in celebration of the coming spring and to welcome the blessing of the Jack of the Green.

Green George's Day

An early spring holiday falling on April 23. The feast of Green George is an ancient Slav festival. In the past, willow trees were cut down and adorned with wreaths, flowers and garlands. Children went from door to door collecting gifts and it was believed that if householders did not give freely, their crops would not grow. Green leaves were associated with this holiday, anticipating the good things to come from the earth.

Kitchen wreath

Kitchen wreaths can be made from culinary herbs which, as they dry, can be removed and used to season foods. Thyme is a good base because it is easy to grow, abundant, and its sweetness lasts long after it has dried. Rosemary, sage, savory, dill and parsley are also good ingredients for a kitchen wreath. Wreaths can be decorated with the edible blossoms of the pot marigold. Kitchen wreaths can also be arranged bound dill stalks.

May Day

May Day, which during the Middle Ages and the Renaissance fell on May 12, is another celebration of the arrival of Spring. In medieval English villages, it was at last warm enough to spend the night in the woods, and young men and women would return in the morning bearing boughs and branches to deck the Maypole. Often a King and Queen were chosen, and adorned with the white blossoms associated with the season, hawthorne, lily of the valley, and daisies.

Daisy Wreath

Daisies are best made into fresh wreaths. Select mature blossoms and insert into a wet sphagnum moss base. A fern is a good companion to these living wreaths suggestive of youth and innocence.

Midsummer Day

Midsummer Day, which falls on June 24, is the celebration of the summer solstice, when the days are longest and the sun highest in the sky. In medieval times, it was considered a time of enchantment when fairies ran rampant in the meadows. It was also the time when marriageable girls were dressed in their finery and paraded before the eligible men. Maidens often wore chaplets composed of white lilies and vervain, and brides were crowned with roses.

Wedding Crown

Brides often wore wreaths as wedding crowns which were dried and passed down as heirlooms. Bridal wreaths can include ribbons, dried blossoms and fragrant herbs with special significance to the season or the bride. Roses were often used because they were associated with love and virtue.

St. Christopher's Day

St. Christopher's Day, celebrated on July 25, is a midsummer holiday of feasting and anticipation of the bounty of August. Because of the abundance of the season, there are many plants which were traditionally associated with this feast day. Among them are, baneberry, osmund fern, and wolves bane, to name just a few.

Herb and Spice Wreath

On a base of artemisia, fragrant herbs may be added in groups of wired bunches of three or four, so that they may be easily removed for use in the kitchen. Attach a ring of bay and in the center, nutmegs, cinnamon and cardamom. Finally, add herbs of significance to you or those you use frequently in the kitchen: caraway, anise, coriander or rue can be tied to the wreath under a velvet bow.

Lammas Day

Lammas Day, August 1, marks the beginning of the harvest season. It was originally a day of worship for the Roman deity Ceres, goddess of the harvest. The first grains of the season were baked into bread on this day, as an offering of thanksgiving. Later, in Christian times, the first fruits of the field were offered to the church.

Wheat is most commonly associated with this holiday.

Lammas Day Wreath

Italian bearded wheat makes an excellent Lammas Day wreath. Attach sheaves to a base of artemisia and decorate with dried calendulas. This wreath makes a delightful front door ornament.

Michaelmas

This harvest festival is celebrated on September 29. This is the height of the drying season. In agrarian times, this was a feast to give thanks for the fruit of the fields. It was also an enchanted time, when townsfolk hung yew, bracken, and other pungent herbs to ward off witchcraft and keep the hearths of home safe as the days grew shorter and winter made its first approach.

Incense Wreath

The most fragrant of wreaths, the incense wreath contains the must unusual materials, and glows with warm autumn colors. On a base of artemisia and sweet grass we add tonka beans, cinnamon sticks and small pieces of sweet smelling sandalwood. To complete the design, we attach a bow and tie in two small bags of frankincense and myrrh. These can easily be removed and burned as incense.

All Hallow's Eve.

All Hallow's Eve falls on October 31, on the eve of All Saint's Day. Historically, All Hallow's Eve was an enchanted time when witches and goblins ruled the night. Witch's wreaths composed of fragrant herbs known for their ability to discourage spirit tricksters, were hung from the rafters, and over thresholds to protect the families within.

Witch's Wreath

The witch's wreath represents the many plants that both attract and repel witchcraft. Some essential plants to use are rue, wild geranium, willow, hawthorne, elder, alder, and rowan tree berries. Oak leaves and vervain were also believed to hinder the witch. Rowan berries add color and extra interest.

St. Martin's Day

St. Martin's Day, falling on November 11, marks the beginning of the Advent season. In Northern Europe, the great Christmas market opens on this day. Traditionally, it was also the time of year that farmers slaughtered their livestock, and salted the winter meat. Feasting, therefore, and fond farewells as workers left for homes or winter jobs, ruled the day.

St. Martin's Day Wreath

A good St. Martin's wreath is a circle of braided straw wrapped with cheerful, embroidered woven binding. Sprigs of boxwood give a festive, holiday look. Lady apples can be wired into the base for color, as they are symbolic of the harvest. A bright bow accented with a sprig of boxwood completes the wreath.

St. Nicholas' Day

St, Nicholas' day is a holiday for those with a sweet tooth. Beautiful cookie molds are used for the famous springerle, or anise cake and baked goods abound. Traditionally, yellow blossoms, such as yarrow or tansy, representing the famous bags of gold that this Dutch saint distributed to the poor, were symbolic of the holiday, and Dutch children would find gold pieces in their shoes on Christmas morning.

St. Nicholas' Wreath

A St. Nicholas' wreath may be made with evergreens or artemisia as a base. Sweet Annie is an appropriate choice, because its gold color is symbolic of the day. You can find cookie molds in a variety of interesting shapes, which make fine decorations for this wreath. To finish, wire bunches of cinnamon sticks and nutmeg, or other spices commonly used to flavor holiday treats.

Harvest and Preservation

The best time to pick material for wreath making is late morning, when the dew has dried but the sun has not yet bleached out colors and essential oils. Flower color is brightest when blossoms first open. Many flowers will continue opening after they have been cut, so watch them closely and cut blooms when they are fully formed.

Heavy stemmed plants, such as willow, bitter sweet or grapevine should be stripped of leaves as soon as they are picked and formed immediately into wreath bases while they are still pliable.

Many herbs can be dried by hanging in bunches. If you won't be using the leaves, strip them from the stems. As plants dry, the stems shrivel and may have to be re-tied. Keep them protected from moisture and light.

Large stems that will be used for wreath bases are best dried in baskets. The stems of artemisia dry into gently curling shapes when dried in this fashion, and are much easier to form into wreaths.

Rosebuds and other flowers that will be wired dry well in a single layer on trays or screens. Place these screens away from light in an airy spot. Decorative seed pods harvested from the garden or the fields can also be dried in this manner.

Many flowers dry best when placed in a drying medium, such as sand, borax, or silica gel. If you

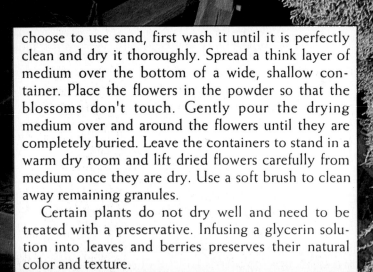

choose to use sand, first wash it until it is perfectly clean and dry it thoroughly. Spread a think layer of medium over the bottom of a wide, shallow container. Place the flowers in the powder so that the blossoms don't touch. Gently pour the drying medium over and around the flowers until they are completely buried. Leave the containers to stand in a warm dry room and lift dried flowers carefully from medium once they are dry. Use a soft brush to clean away remaining granules.

Certain plants do not dry well and need to be treated with a preservative. Infusing a glycerin solution into leaves and berries preserves their natural color and texture.

Making a Wreath Base

To construct an artemisia base, use stems of silver king with the curling tops removed. Begin by bending the stems evenly around the wire frame, securing them together with wire as you go. Do not wire them too tightly. You will need room to insert springs of the silver tips into the base. Cover the back of the base with strands of artemisia to give it a finished look.

When you are satisfied with your base, begin to cover it by inserting the feather tips of the artemisia branches. You may use individual sprays or prepared bundles. Turn the curls toward the center, working clockwise until the circle is filled. Shape the outside line carefully as you work in order to maintain a good circle. Control stragglers by wrapping wire lightly around the whole wreath and then covering the wire with more artemisia sprays.

Decorating

After the base is completed, you are ready to add decorative material. If you are using weak stemmed flowers, wire them before inserting them into your wreath with lightweight florist's wire. Gently but firmly push the end of the wire into the base of the bloom; hold the base of the bloom in one hand, and gradually twist the wire around the stem of the flower; then it is ready to insert into the wreath base. Push your wired or stiff stemmed flower firmly into the base.

If you are using spices, they need to be pierced and wired. Use a small bit to drill holes in nutmeg and cinnamon; then wire them together in bunches of three with florist's wire. Cardamom can be pierced with a sturdy needle or stiff wire.

To add little bags of spices or potpourri, twist them closed with fine wire and attach them under the bow of the wreath. To make a hangar for your wreath, twist a piece of wire to form a small loop in the center. Then work the ends of the wire into the framework of the wreath to secure them.

Living Wreath

A living wreath is made on a special wire frame which must be packed with sphagnum moss and soaked thoroughly with water. Then begin inserting plants.

Living wreaths must be put on trays to hold moisture and to make watering possible. If kept moist, a living wreath lasts almost indefinitely. Water the moss at least once a week.

Making Garlands

To make a garland, start by braiding together wild flowers, such as daisies, with ferns and grasses. Insert clusters of clovers and daisies into each strand; they will create a lovely background for other flowers you may wish to add.

You may also bind a few stems of flowers or grasses together with fine wire. Knot the wire firmly around the stems, take several turns around the length of the stems, and finish with a knot, but do not cut the wire. Position a second bunch of flowers over the stems of the first and continue, first tying a knot, then wrapping the stems, this time joining the stems of both bunches. Secure it with a knot before adding a third bunch. Proceed until the flower rope is of desired length.

Tools and Supplies

WIRE FRAMES: Wire rings are readily available and inexpensive, so we suggest purchasing rather than making one. When you are choosing your ring size, bear in mind that to the frame dimension, you will add two or three inches of material. For living wreaths, you will need a wire frame made with four concentric circles of wire cross-braced with wire so that they have some height or depth. Ten-inch frames or larger work best.

WIRE: of various weights and types is an absolute necessity. You will need green-coated, florist's's wire for binding evergreens, and silver wire for artemisia and statice.

WIRE CUTTER AND STEM CUTTER, may be combined in a single tool if you can find one. The one we use at Caprilands was originally an electrician's tool and works efficiently for both purposes.

A GLUE GUN is helpful when you need to place small, unruly bits into a design.

AN ELECTRIC DRILL is necessary for whole spices and these materials must be drilled before being attached to the wreath.